I0463620

MANDALA

Adult Coloring Book

Dover Design Coloring Books

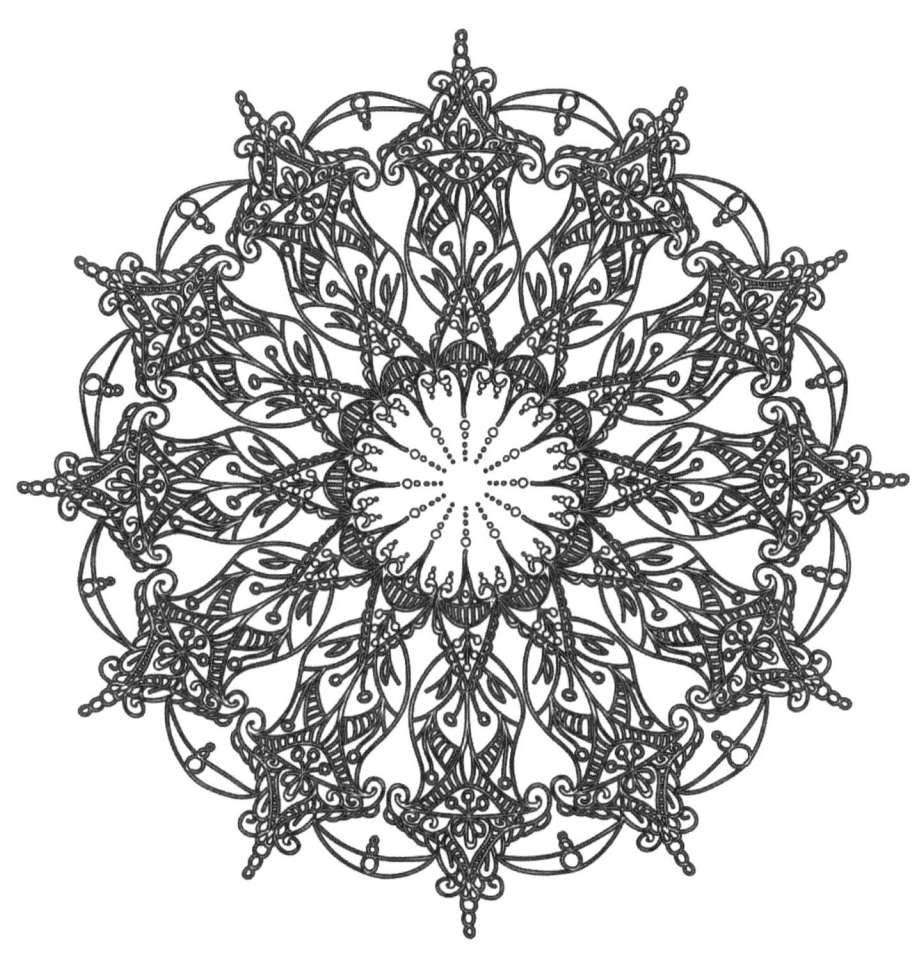

TOONING ARTWORK

MANDALA

Adult Coloring Book

Dover Design Coloring Books

Copyright: Published in the United States by Tooning

Published December 2016

ISBN-13:
978-1544142241

ISBN-10:
1544142242

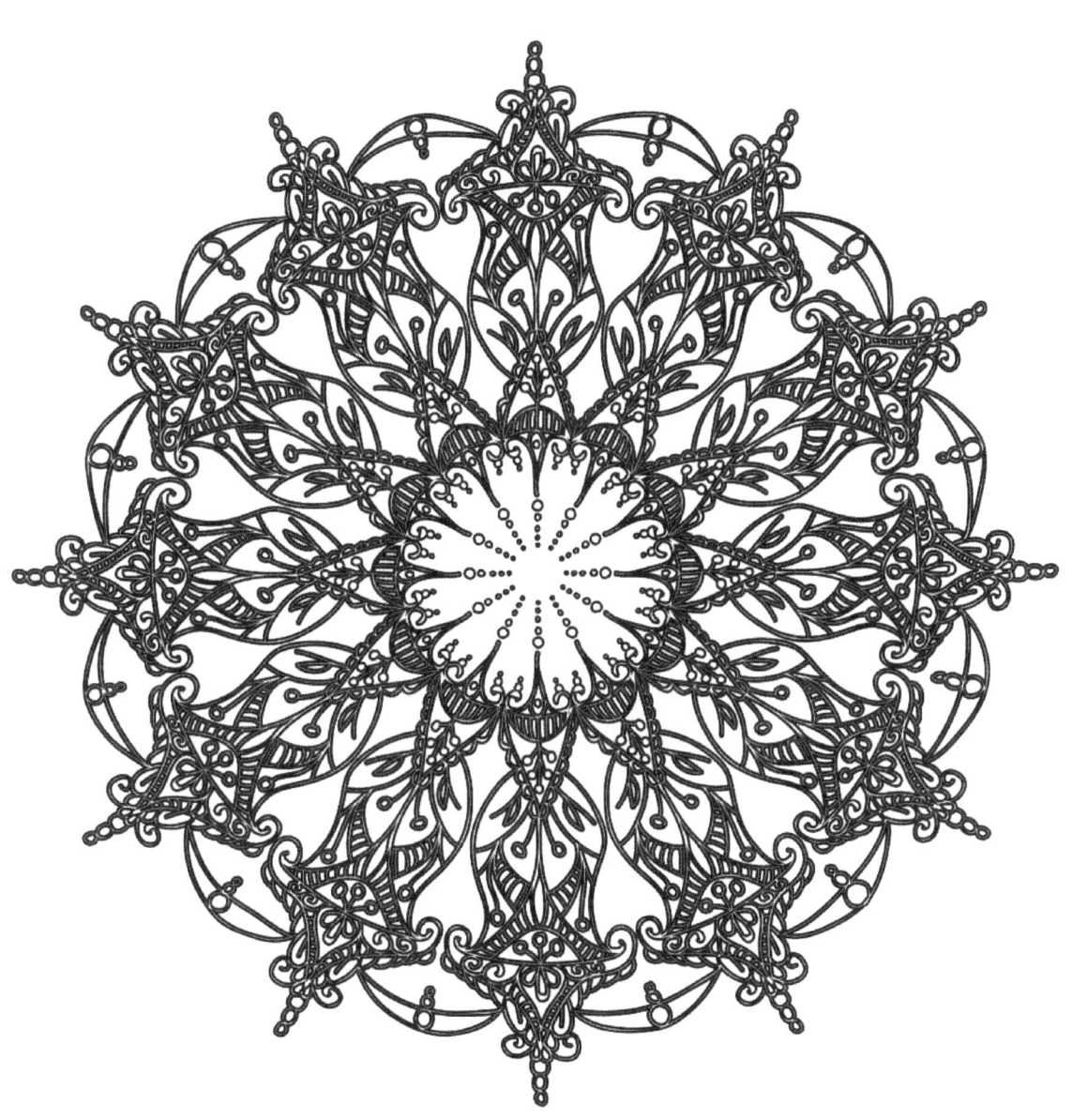

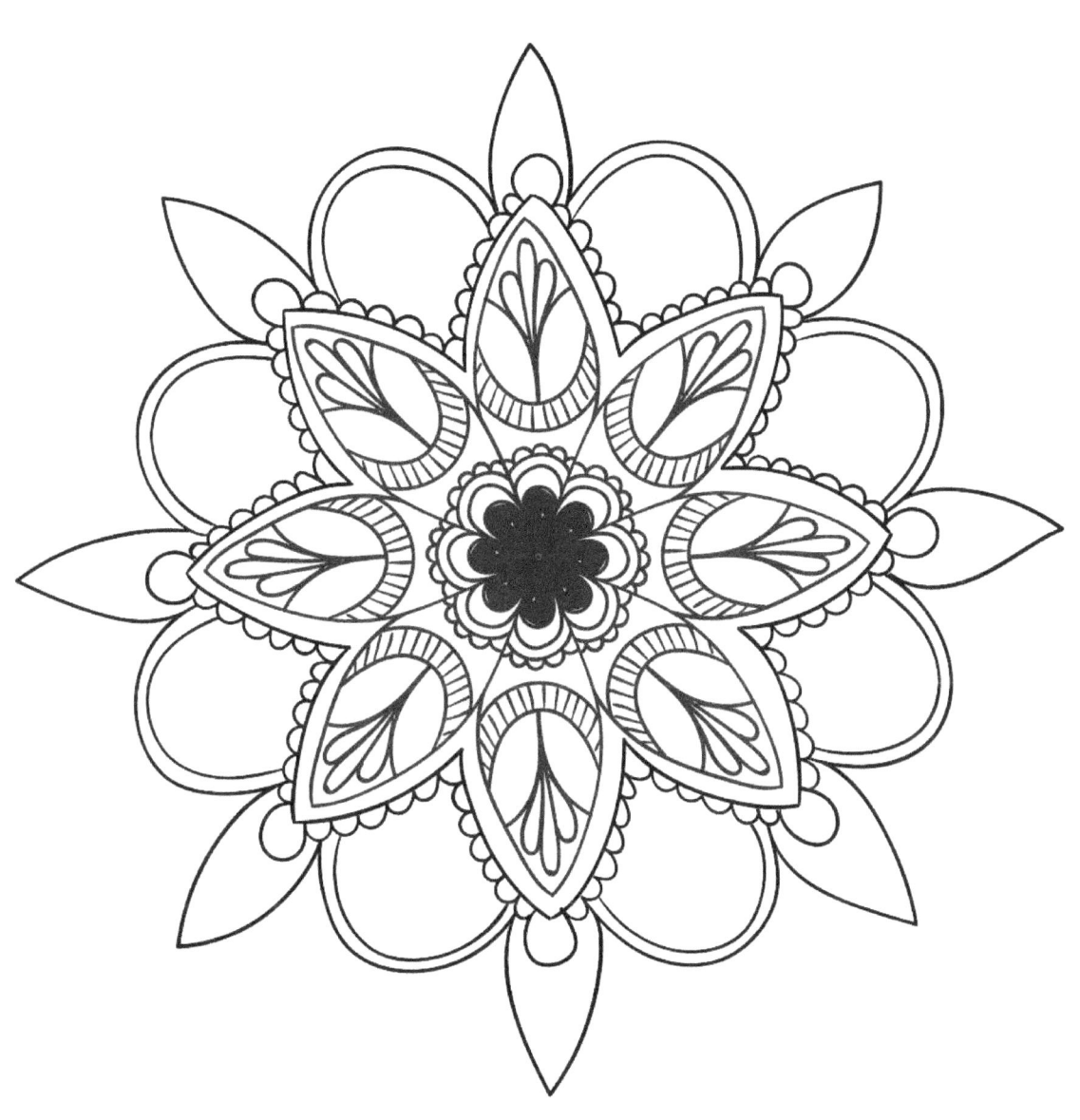

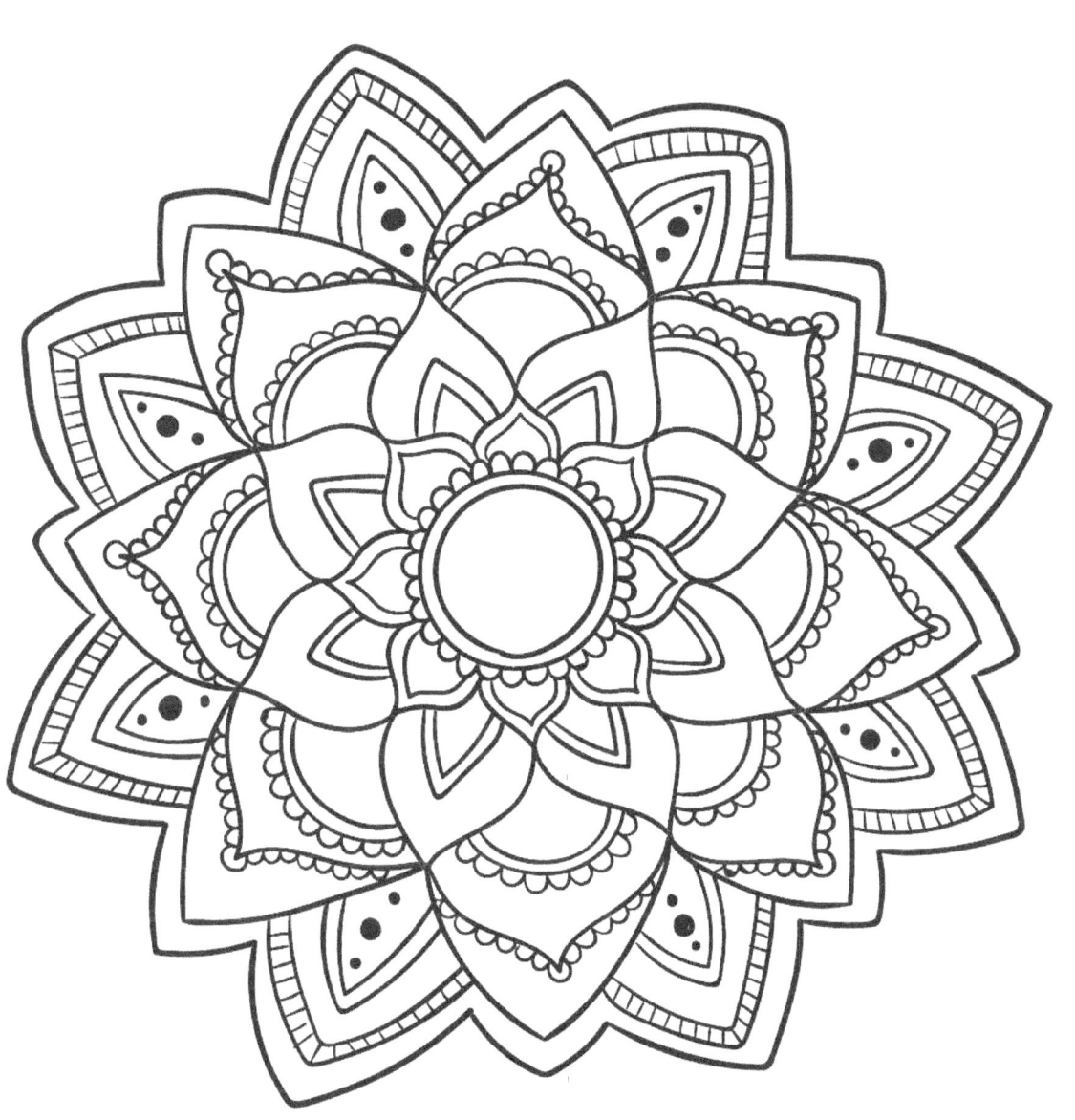

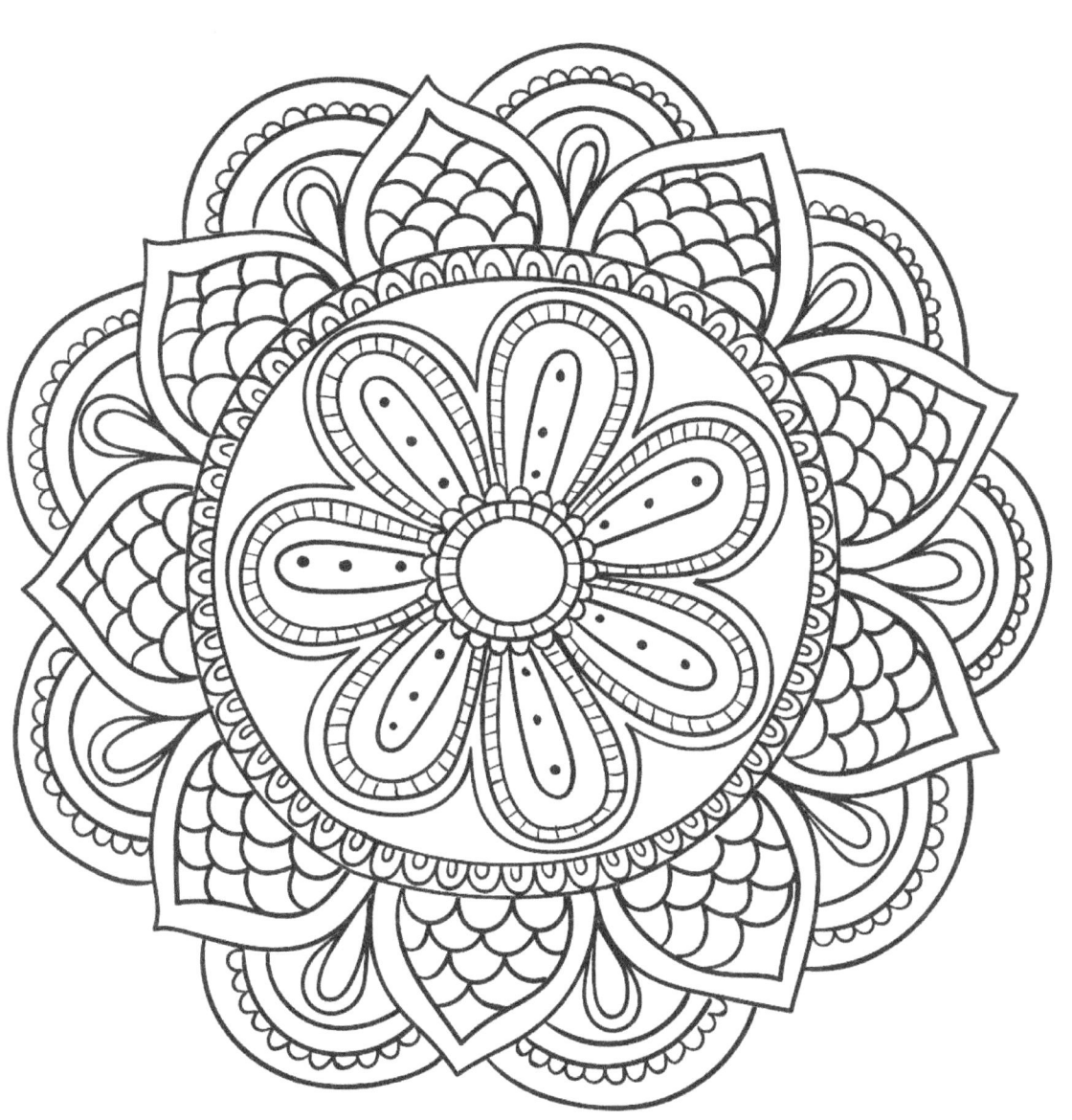

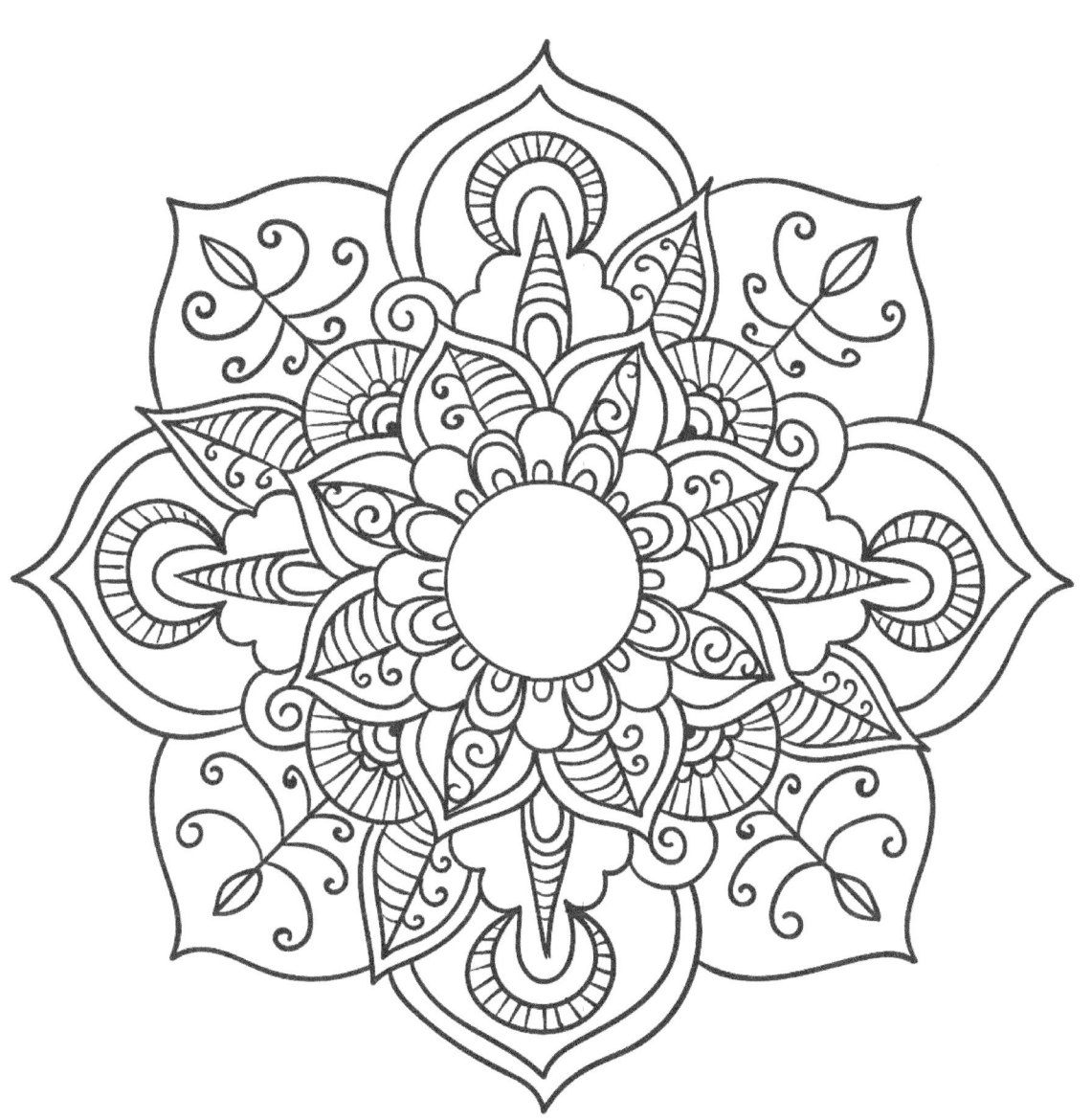

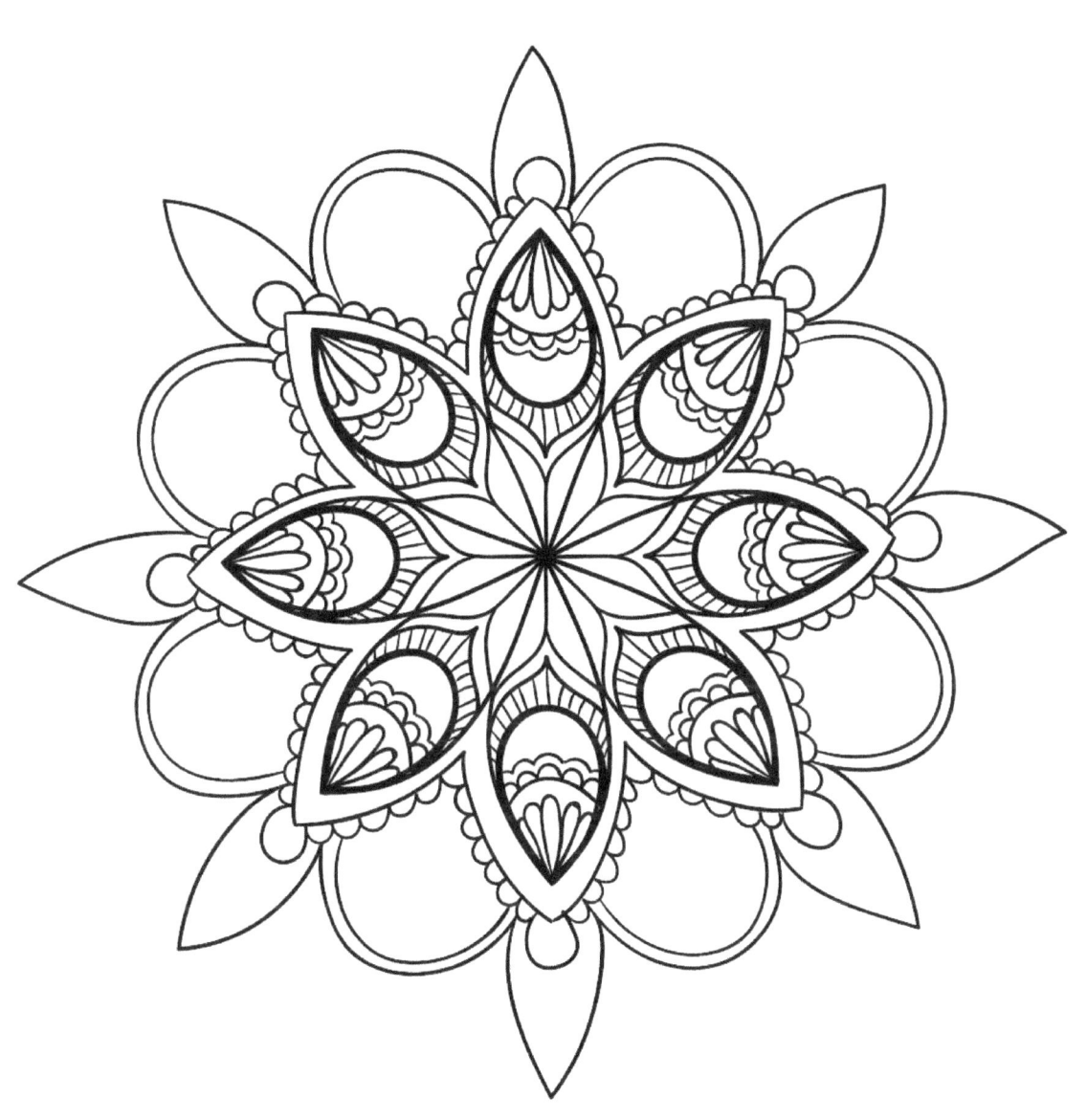

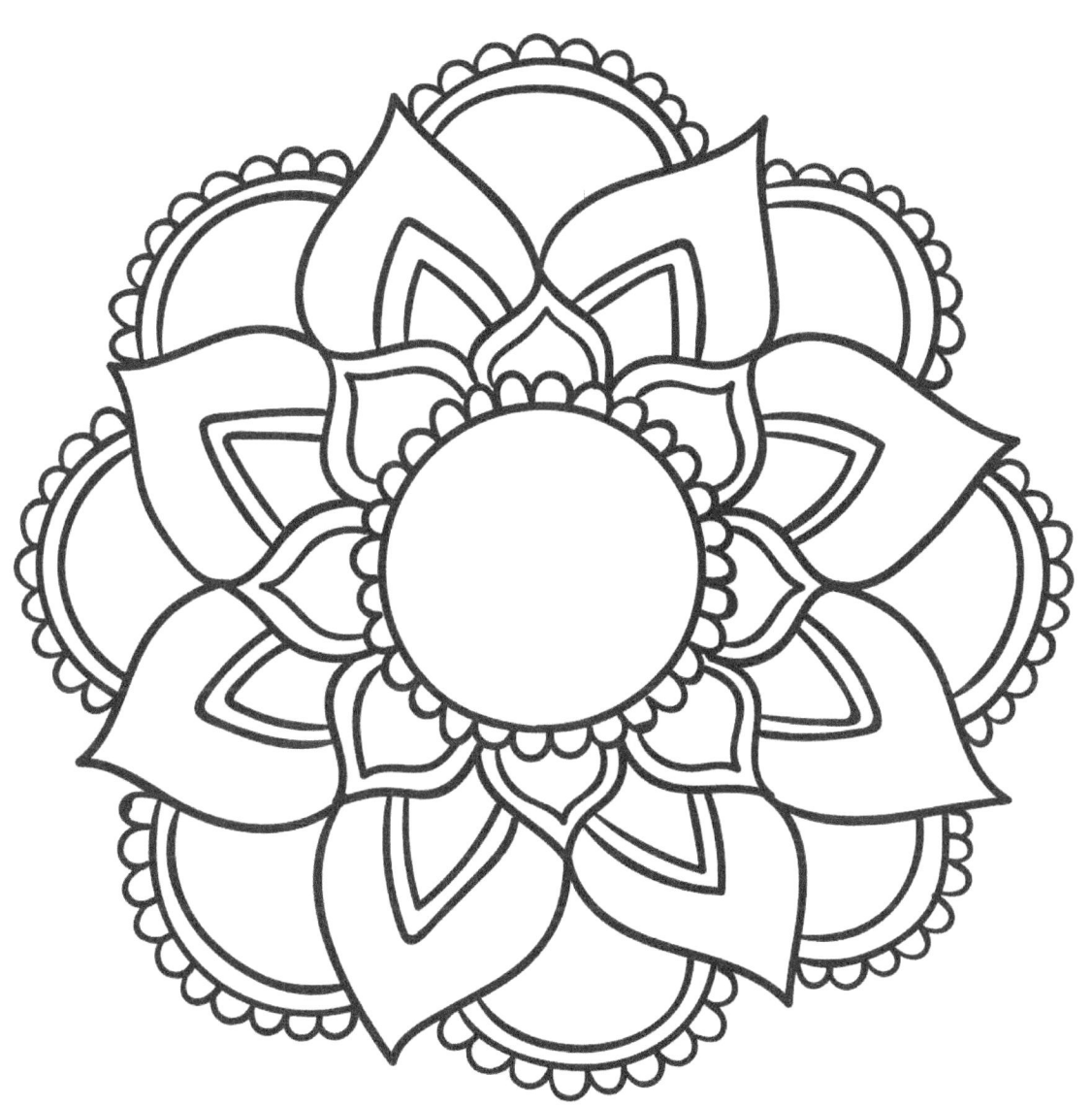

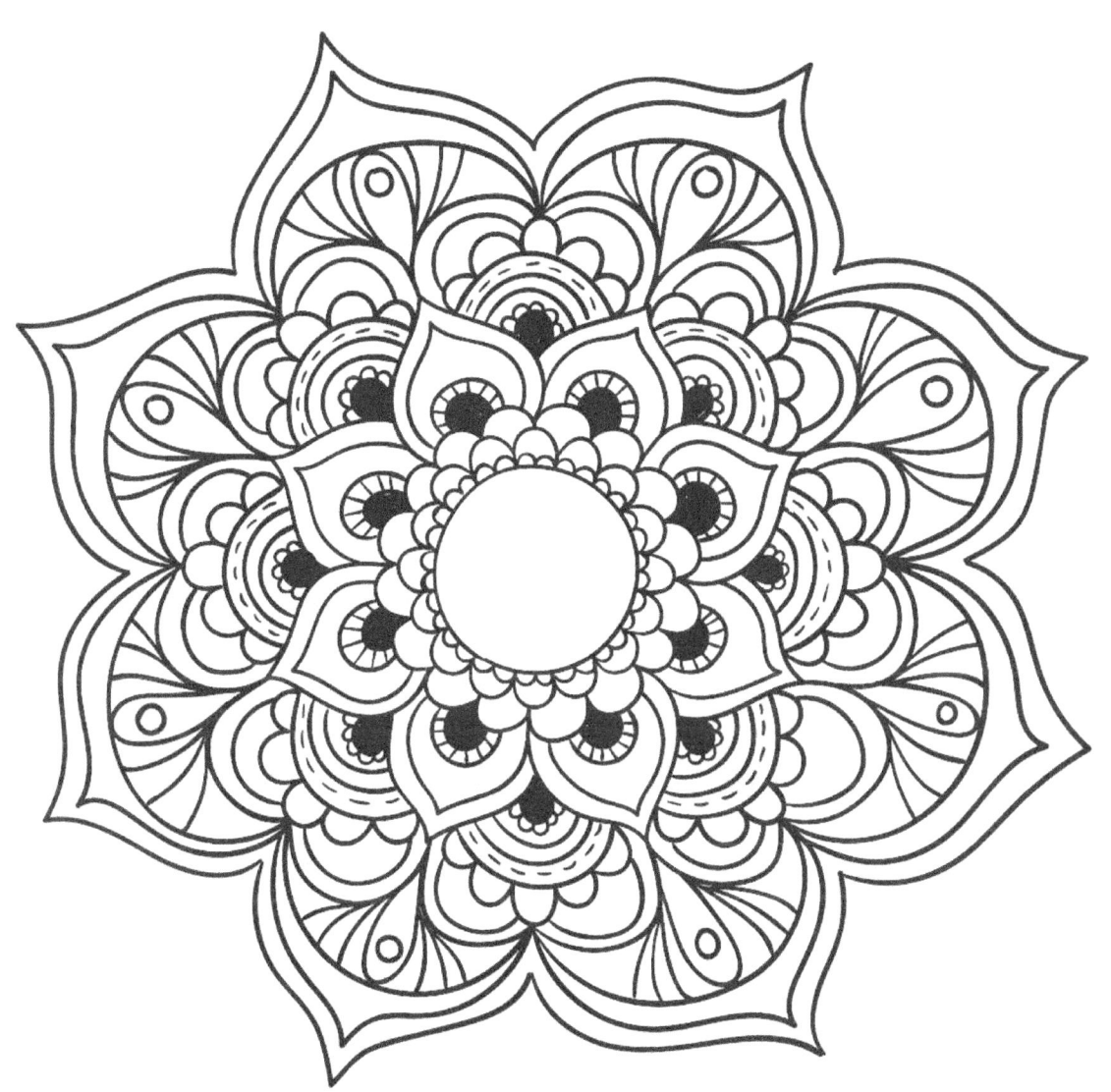

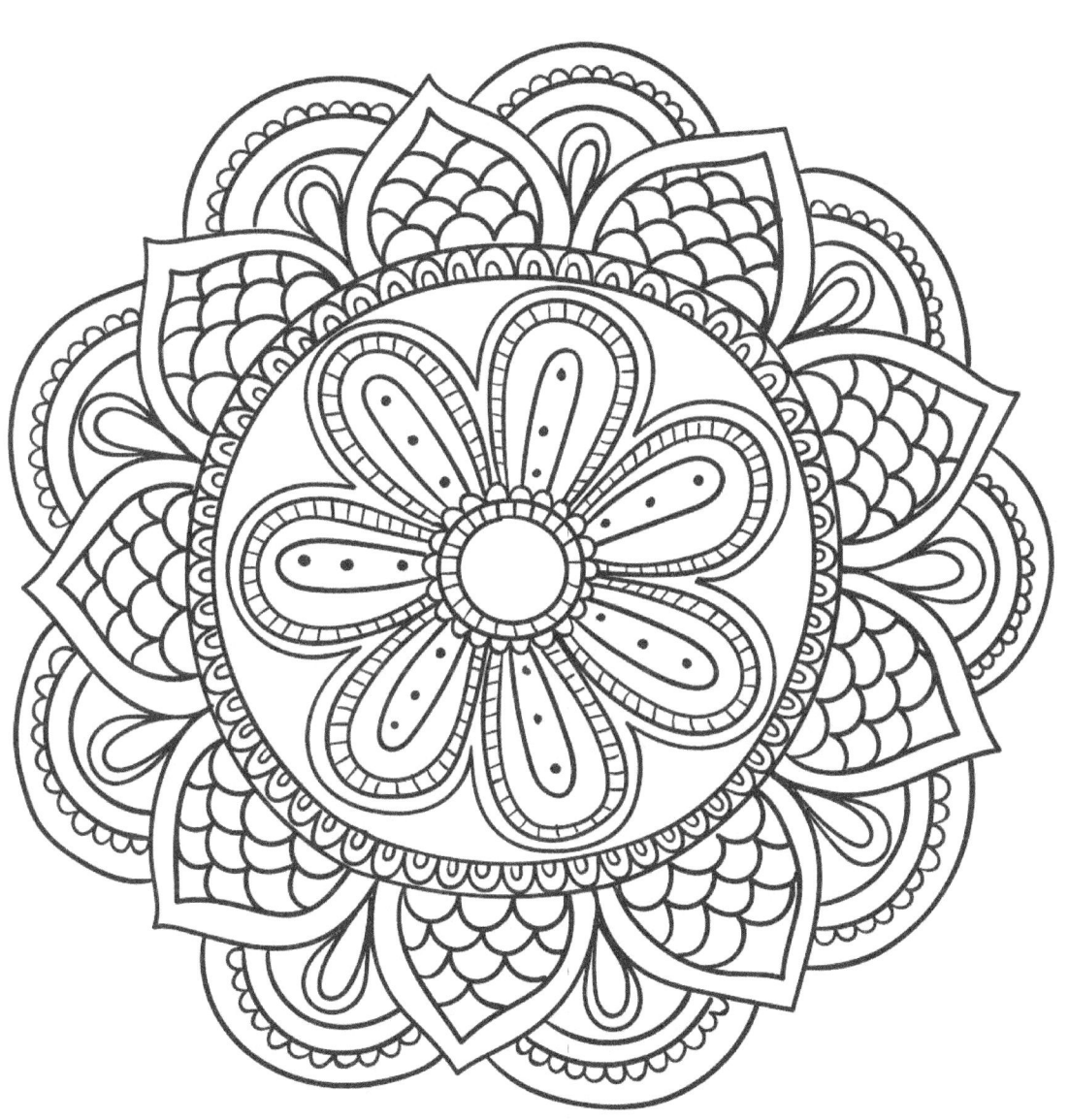

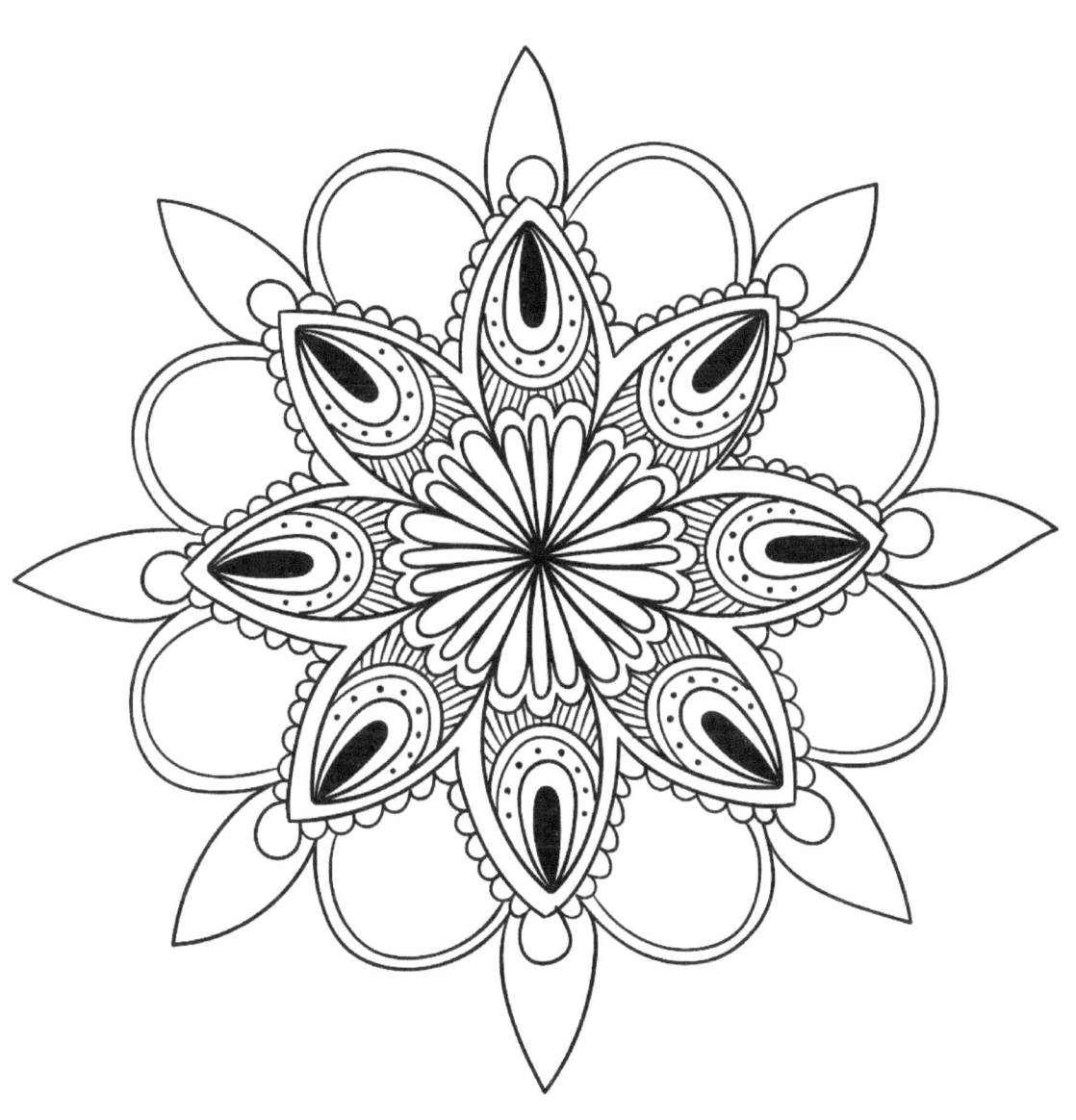

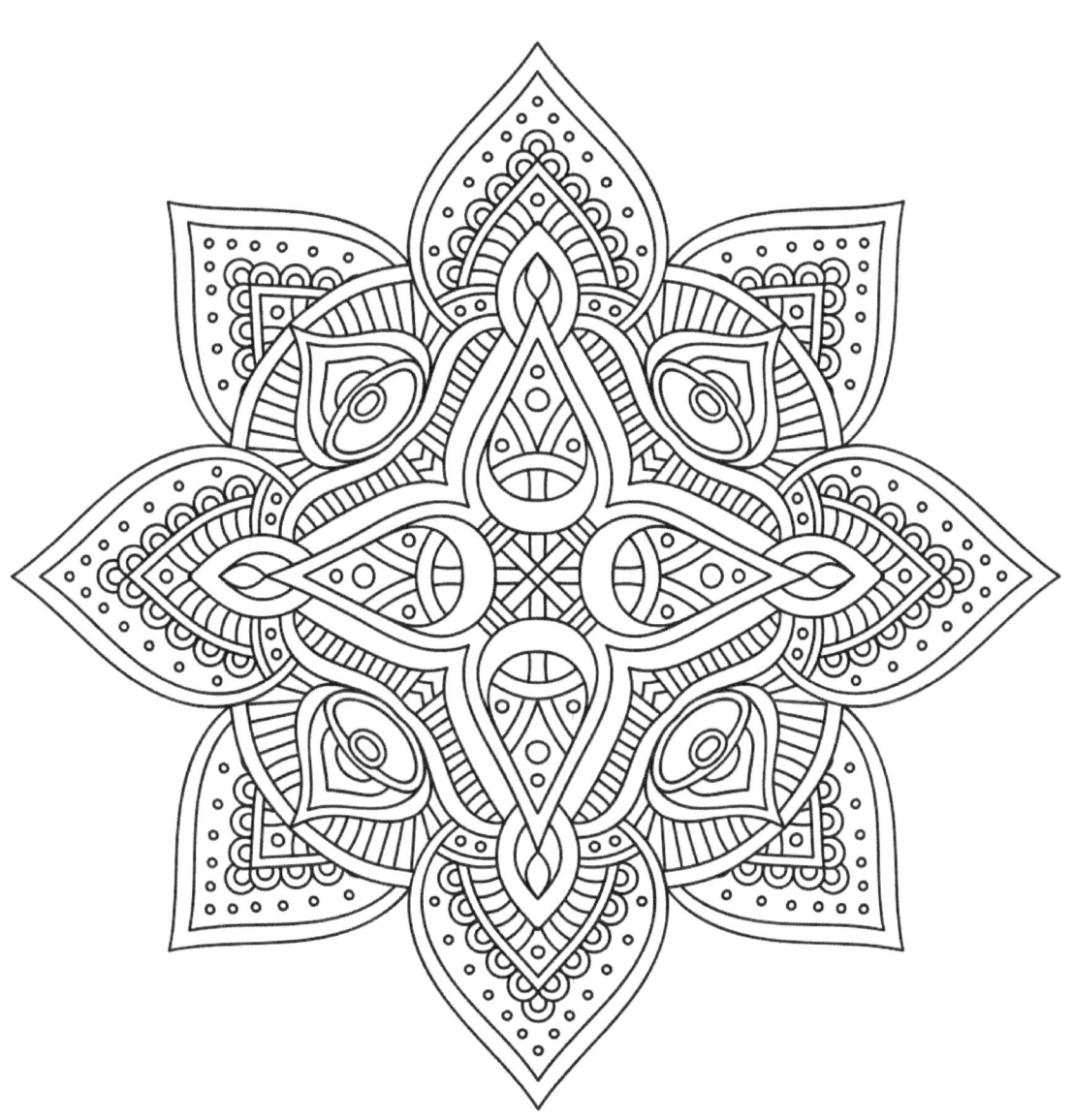

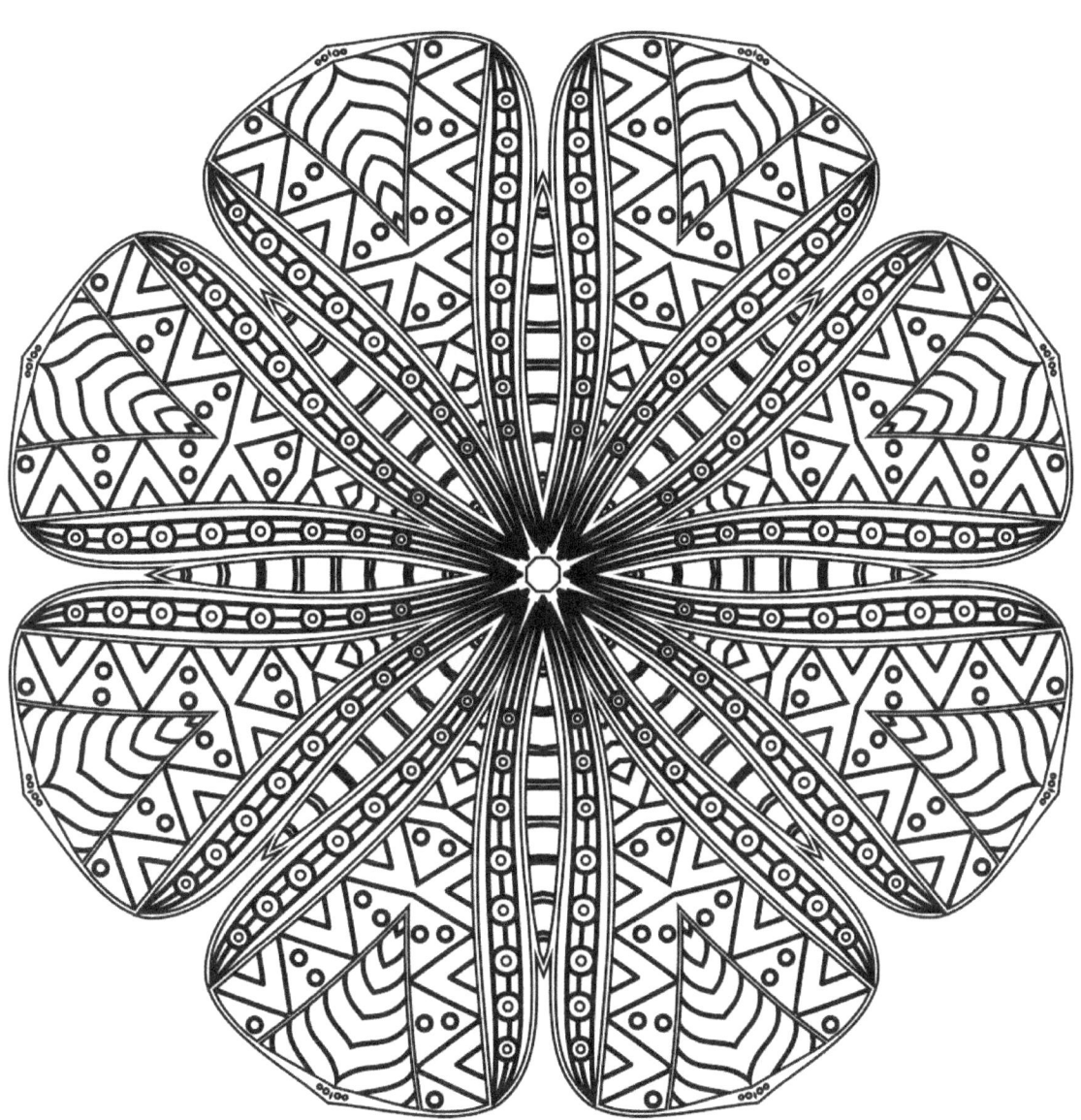

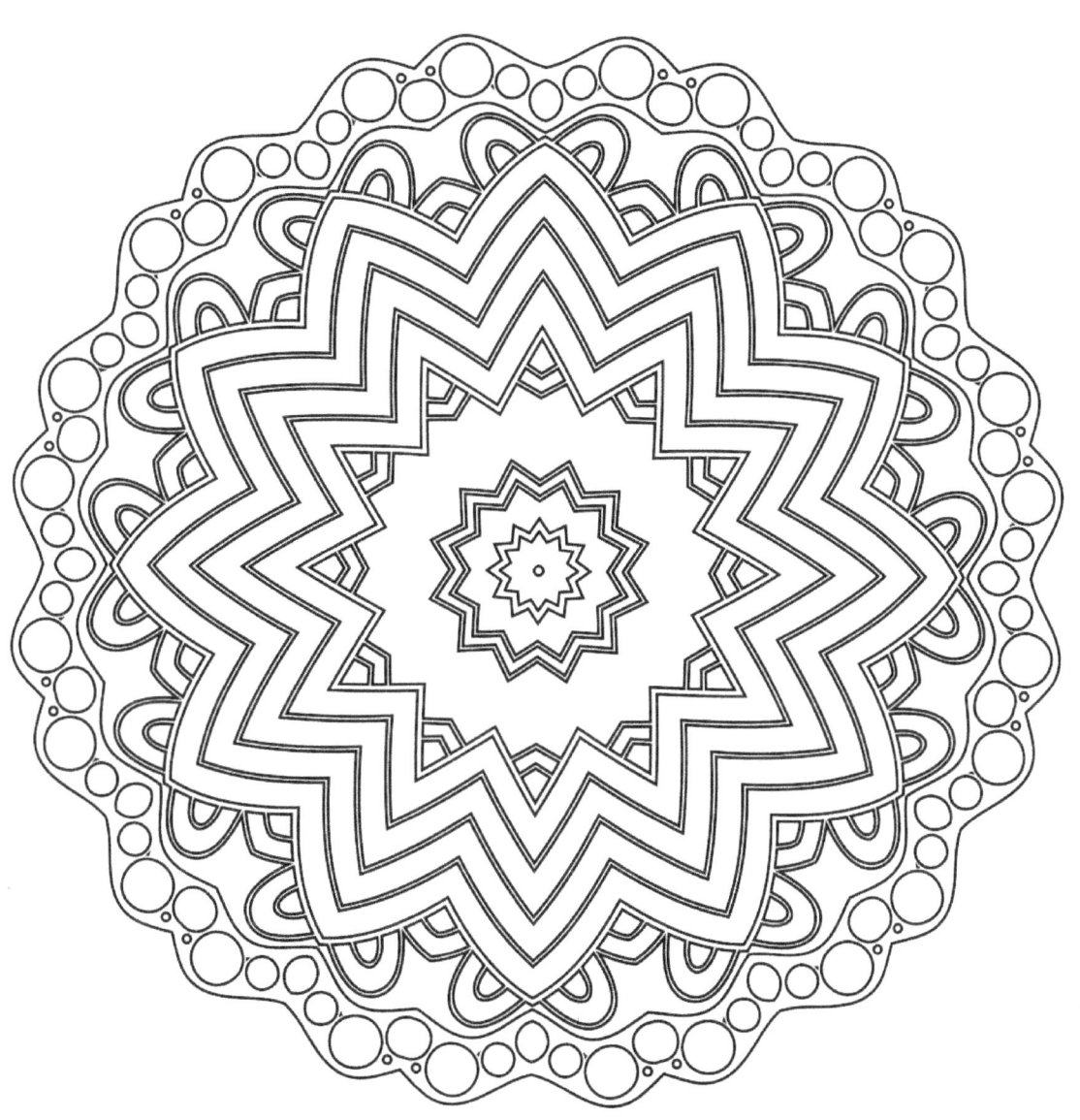

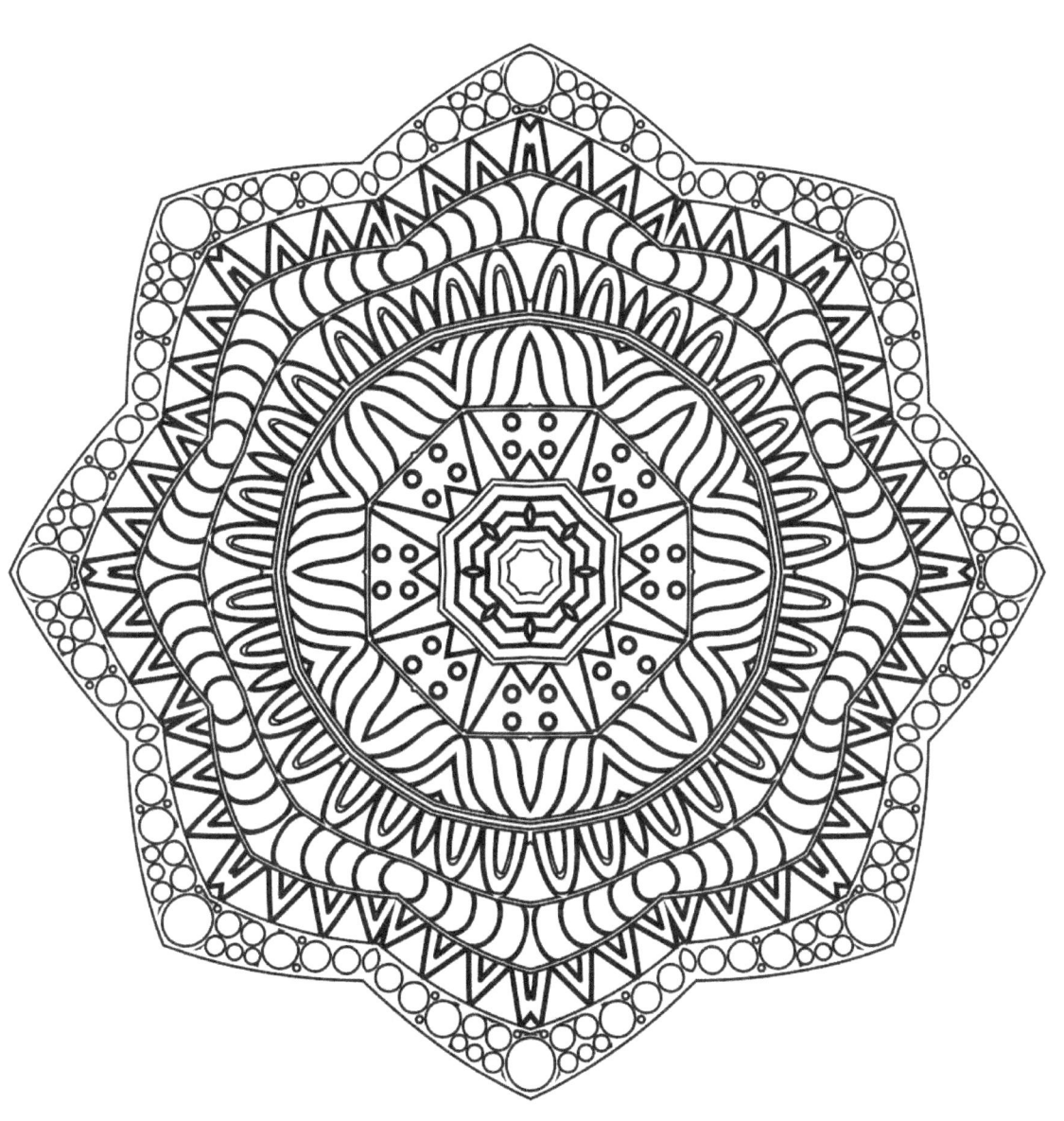

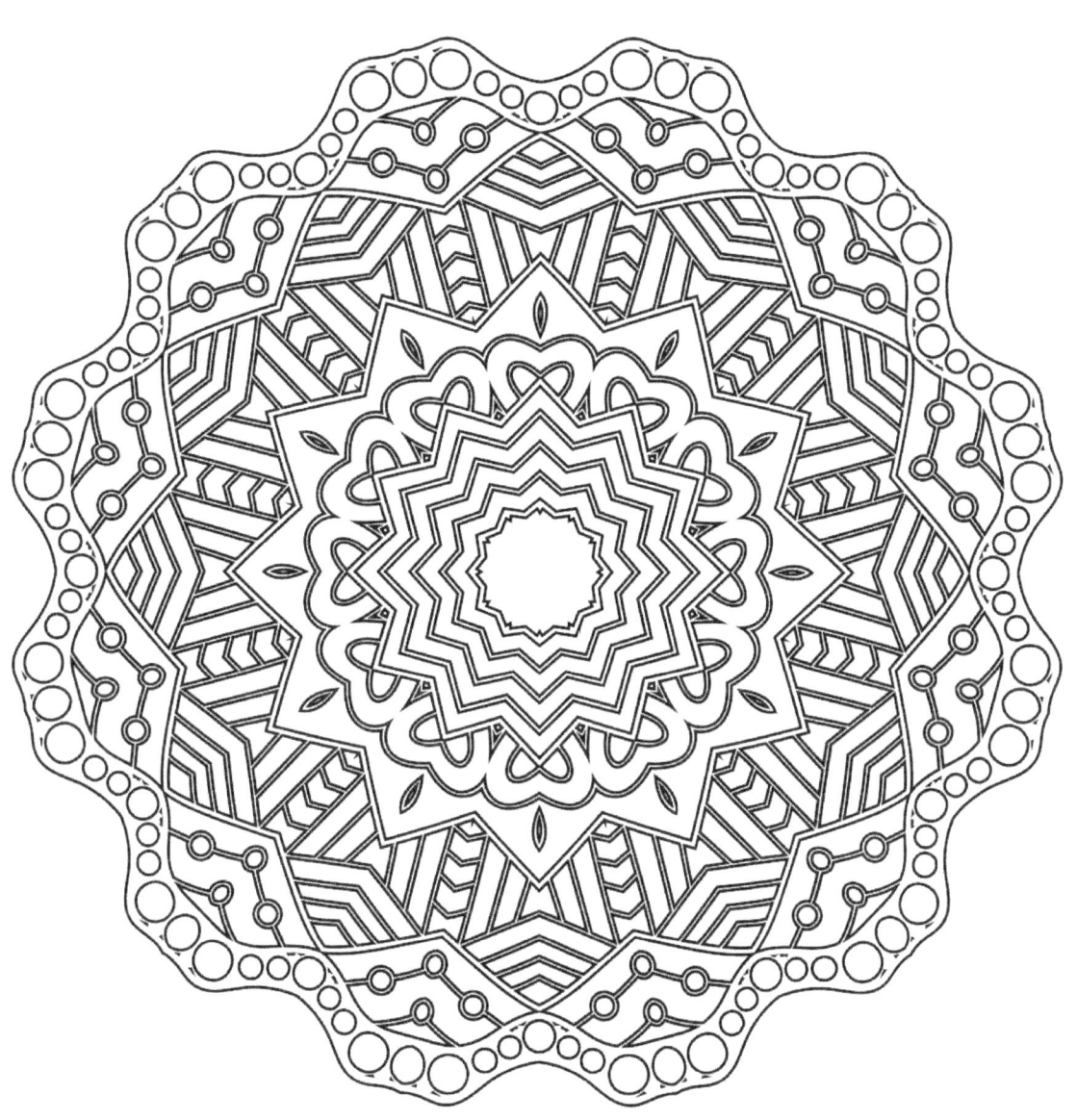

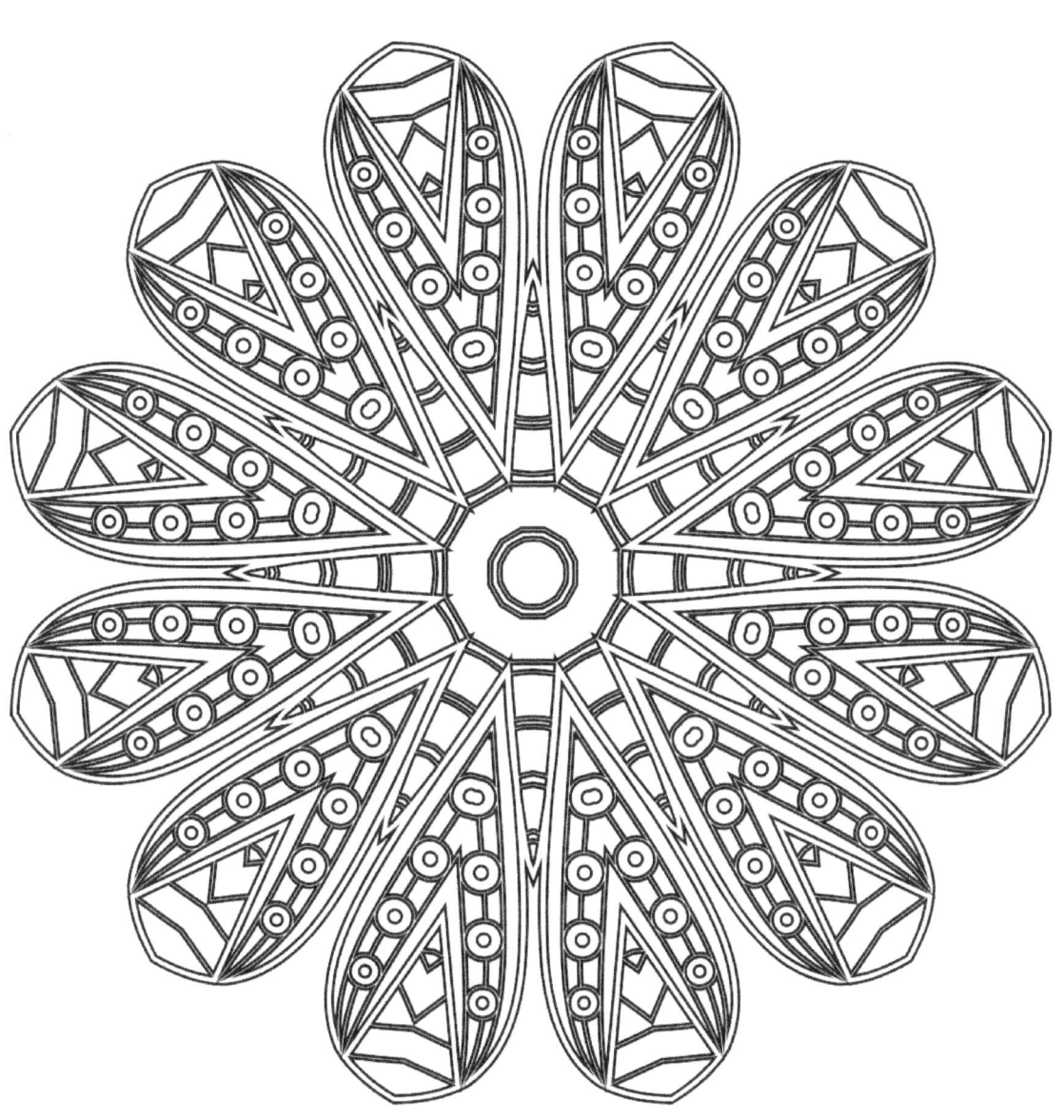

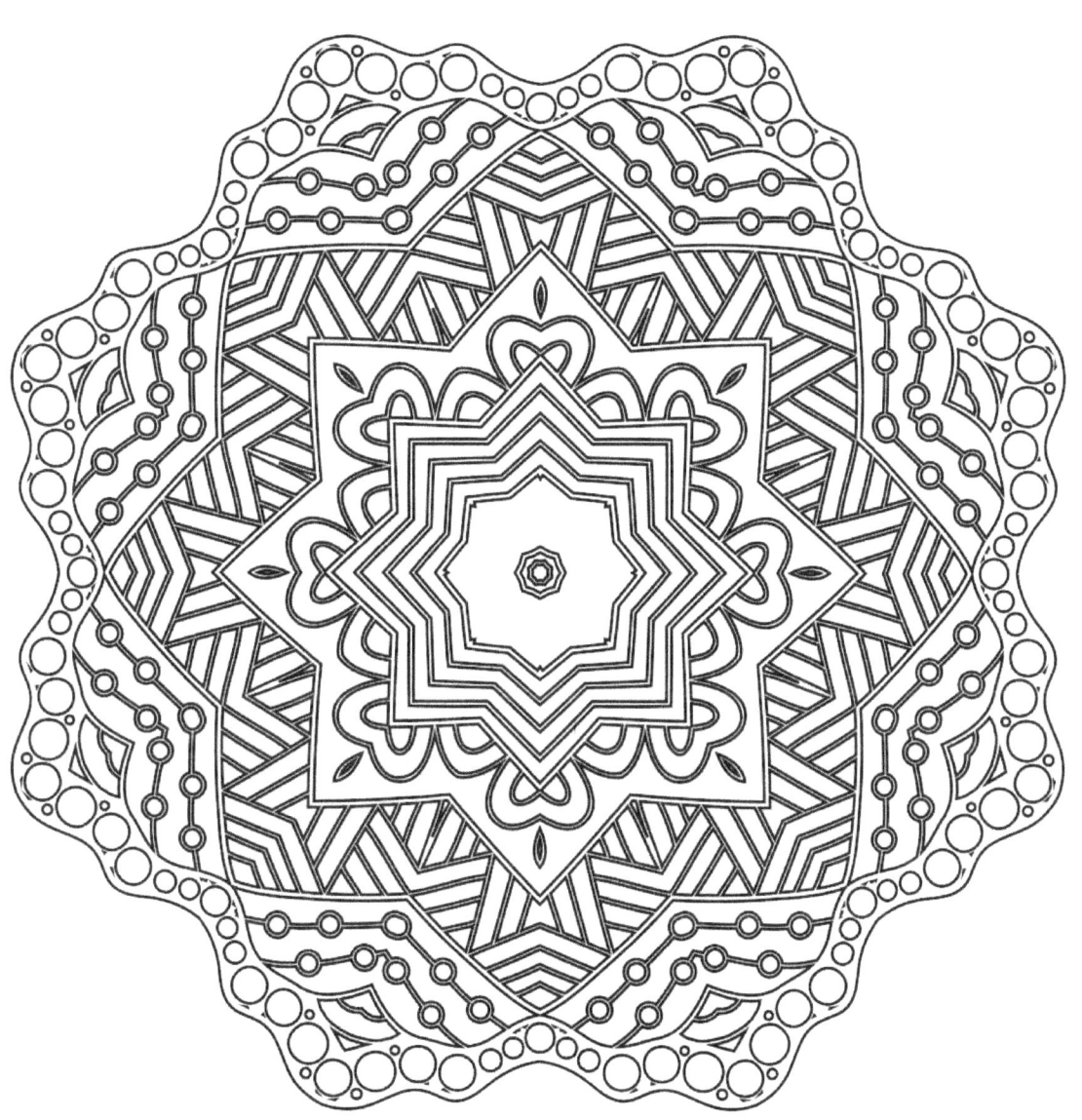

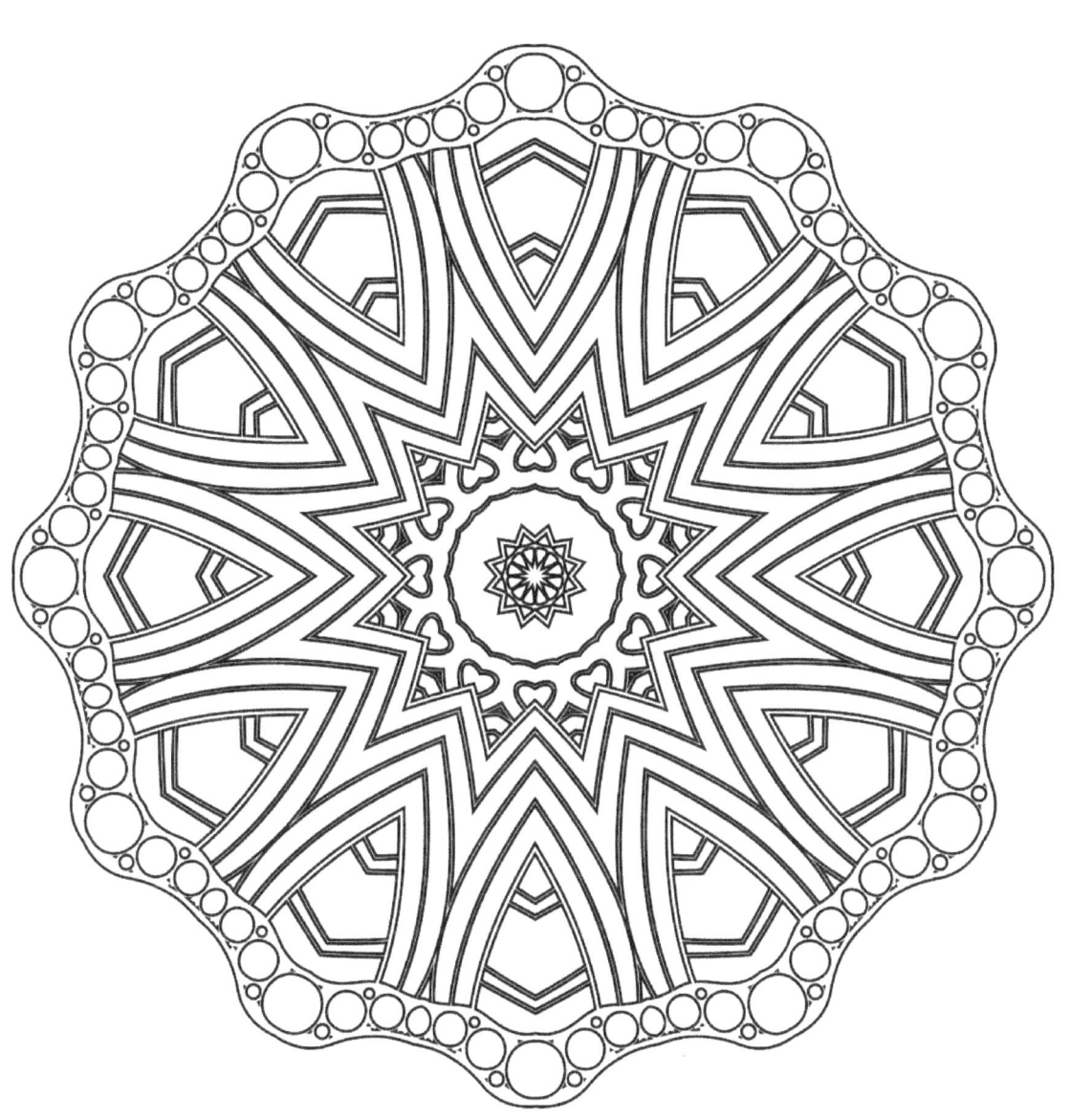

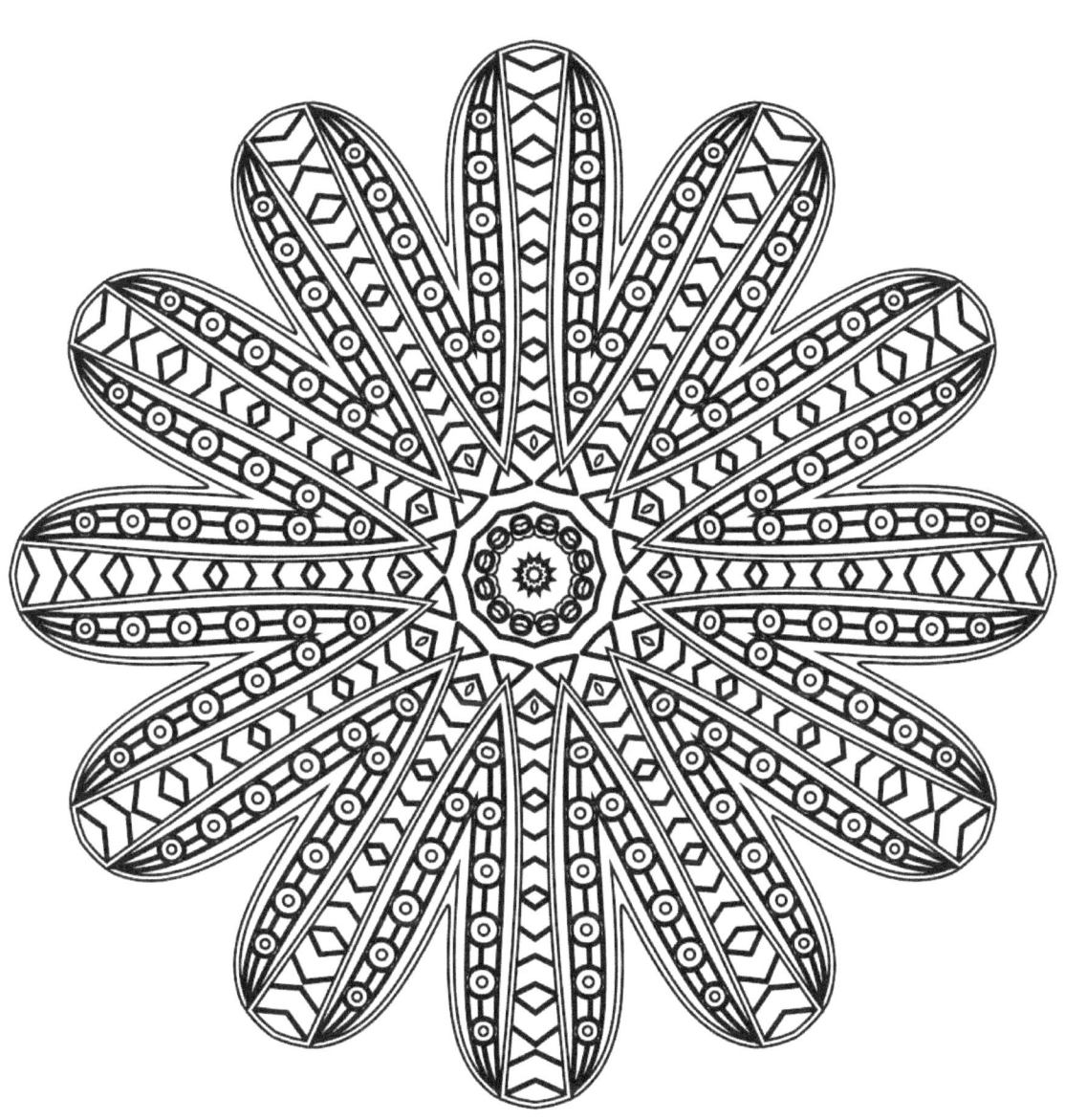

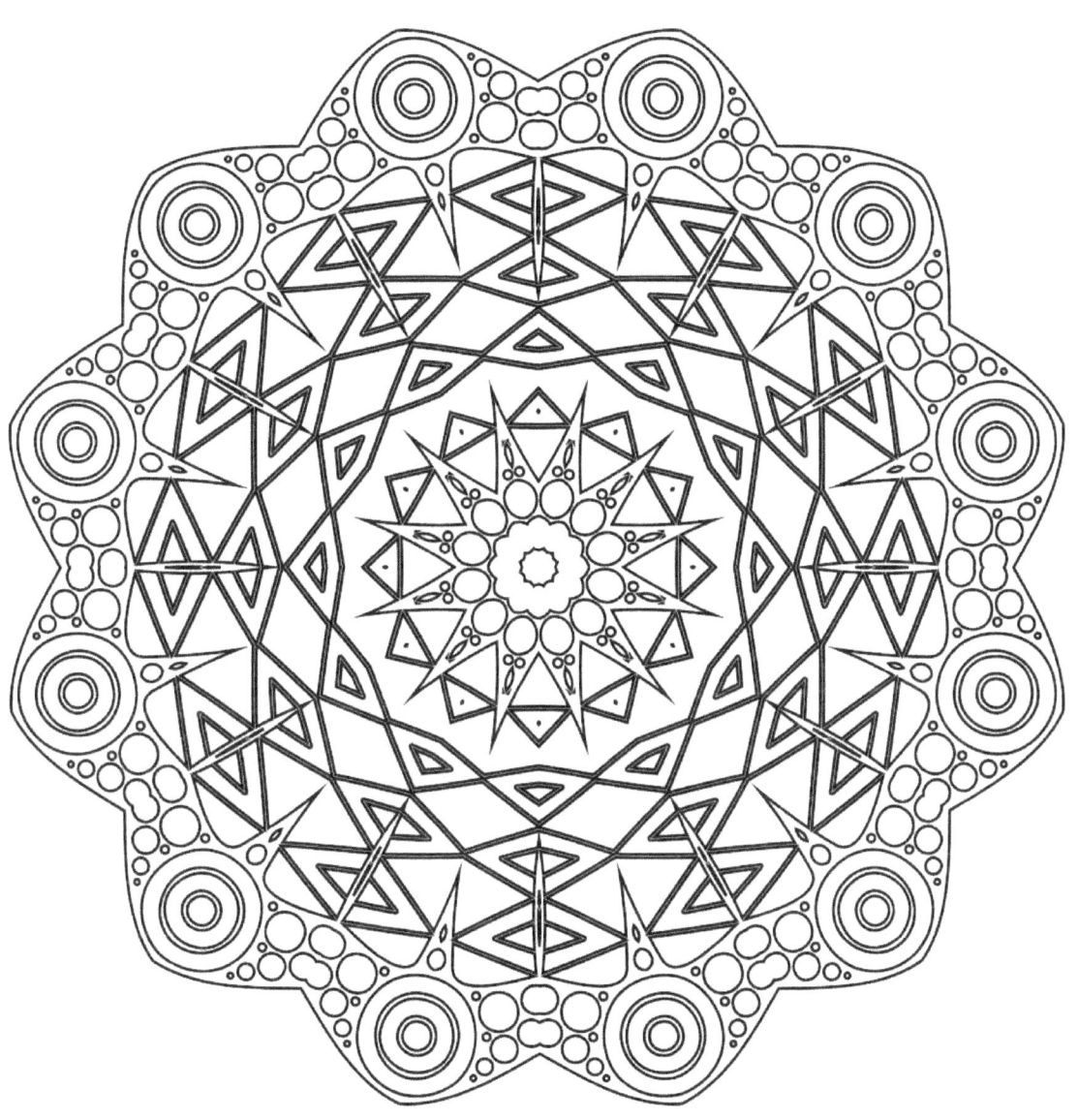

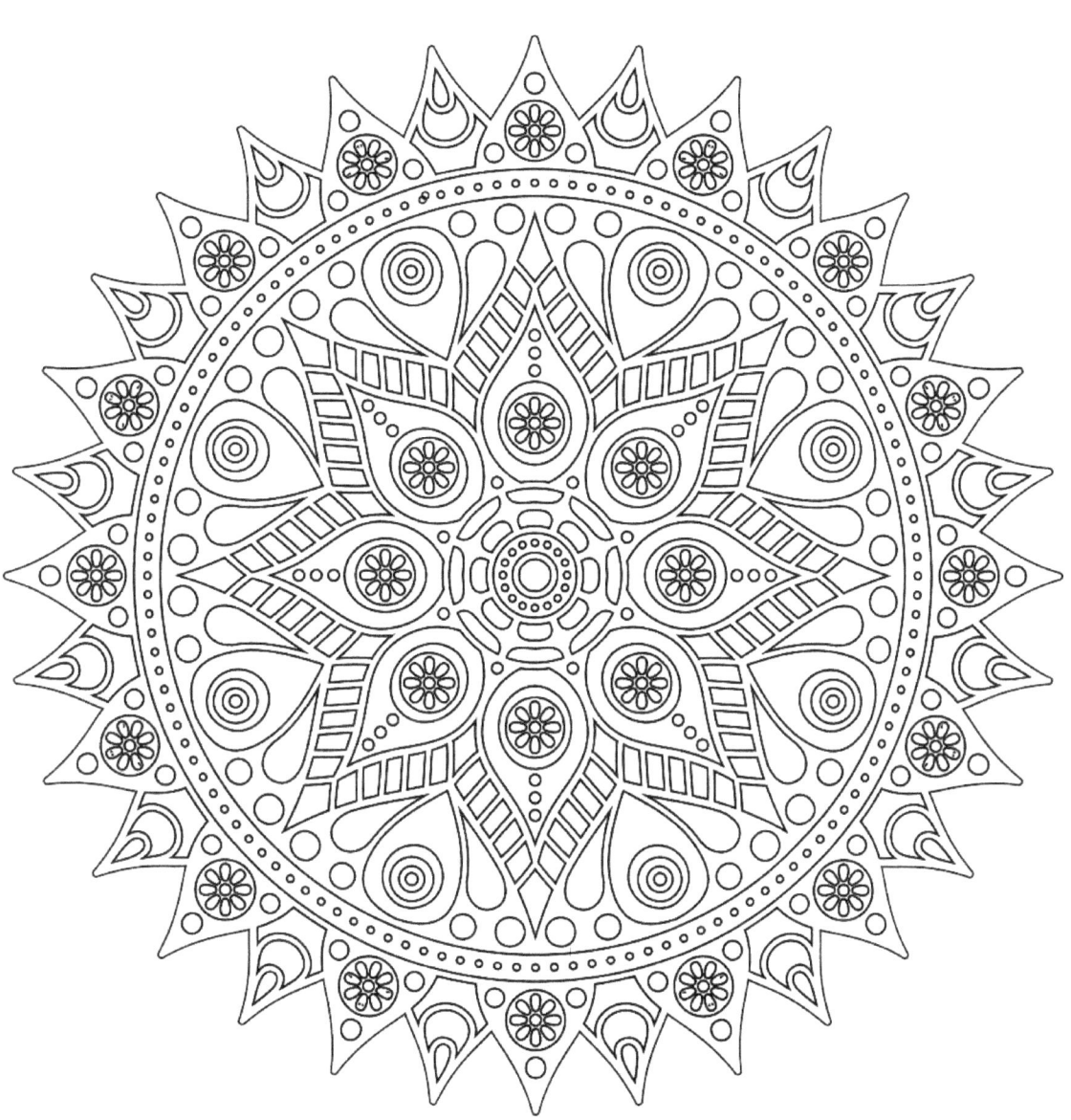

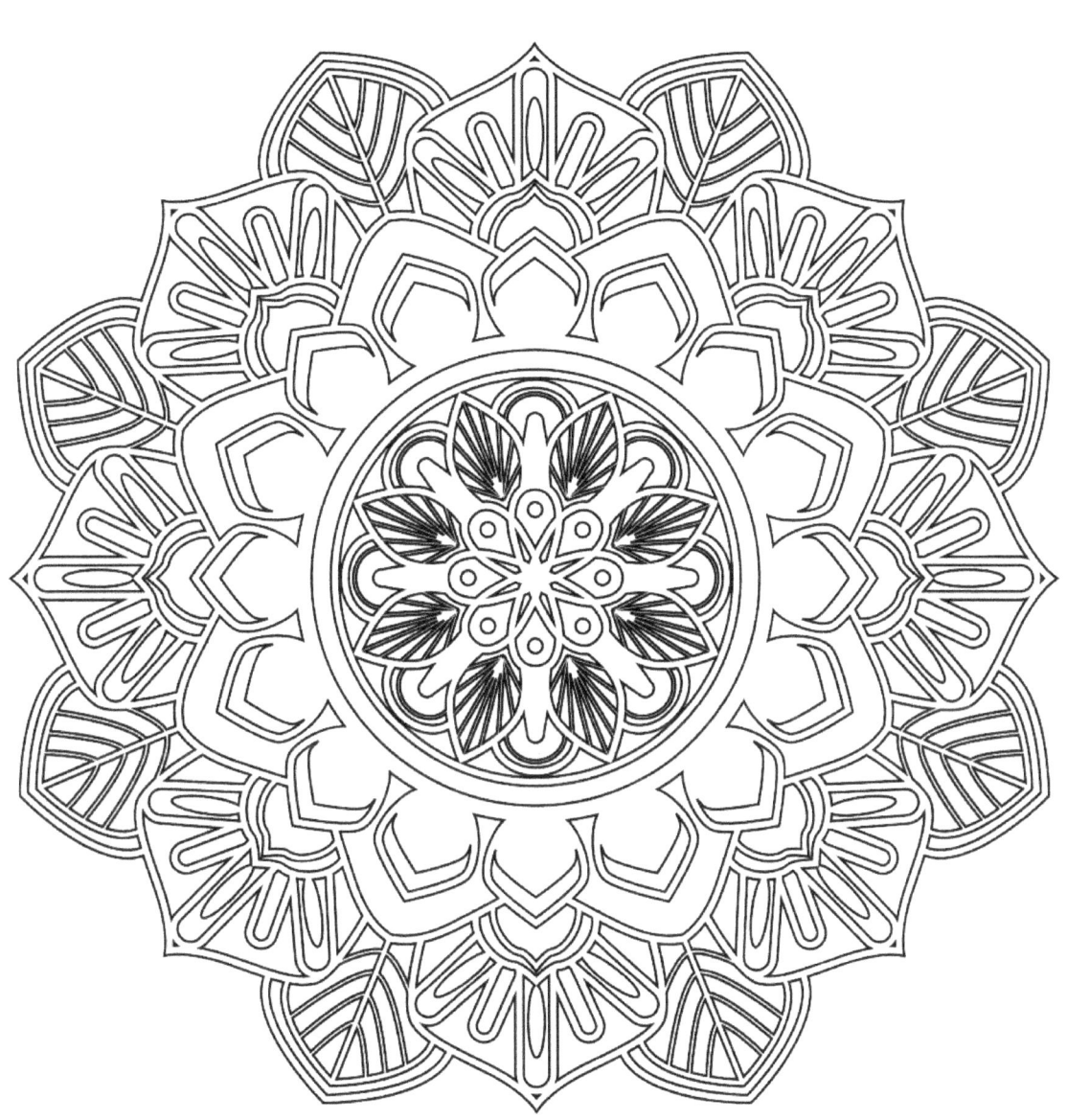

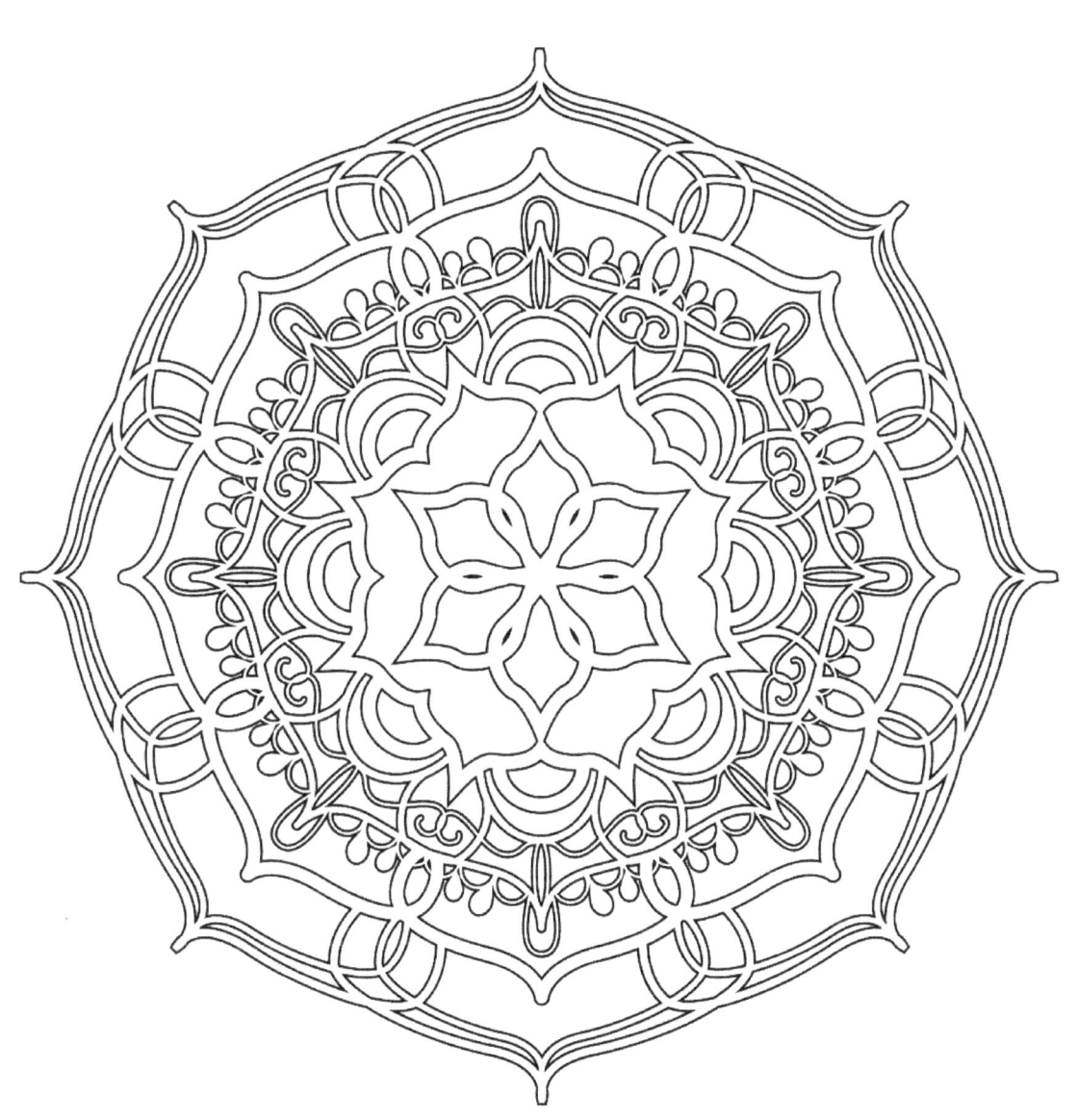

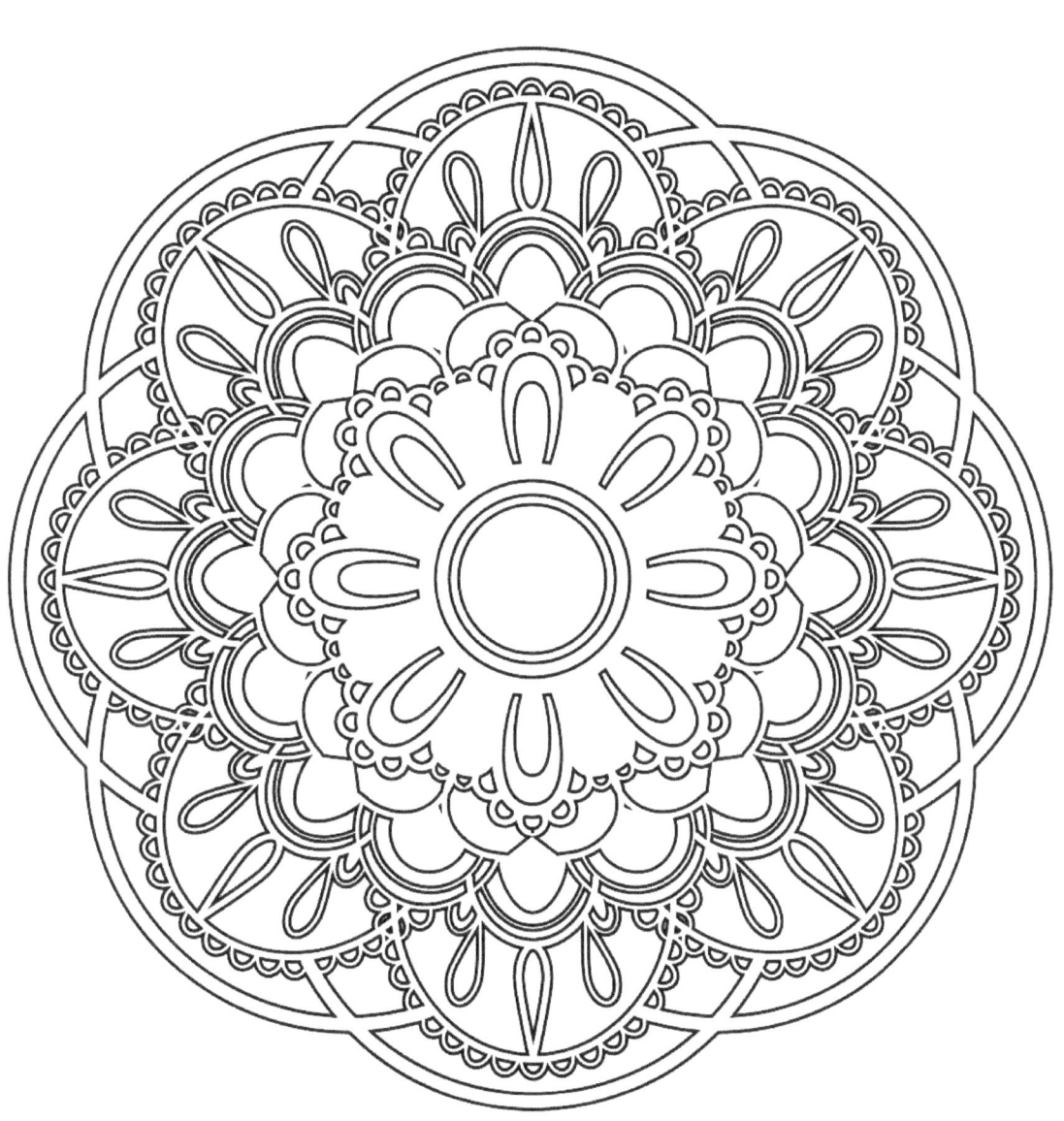

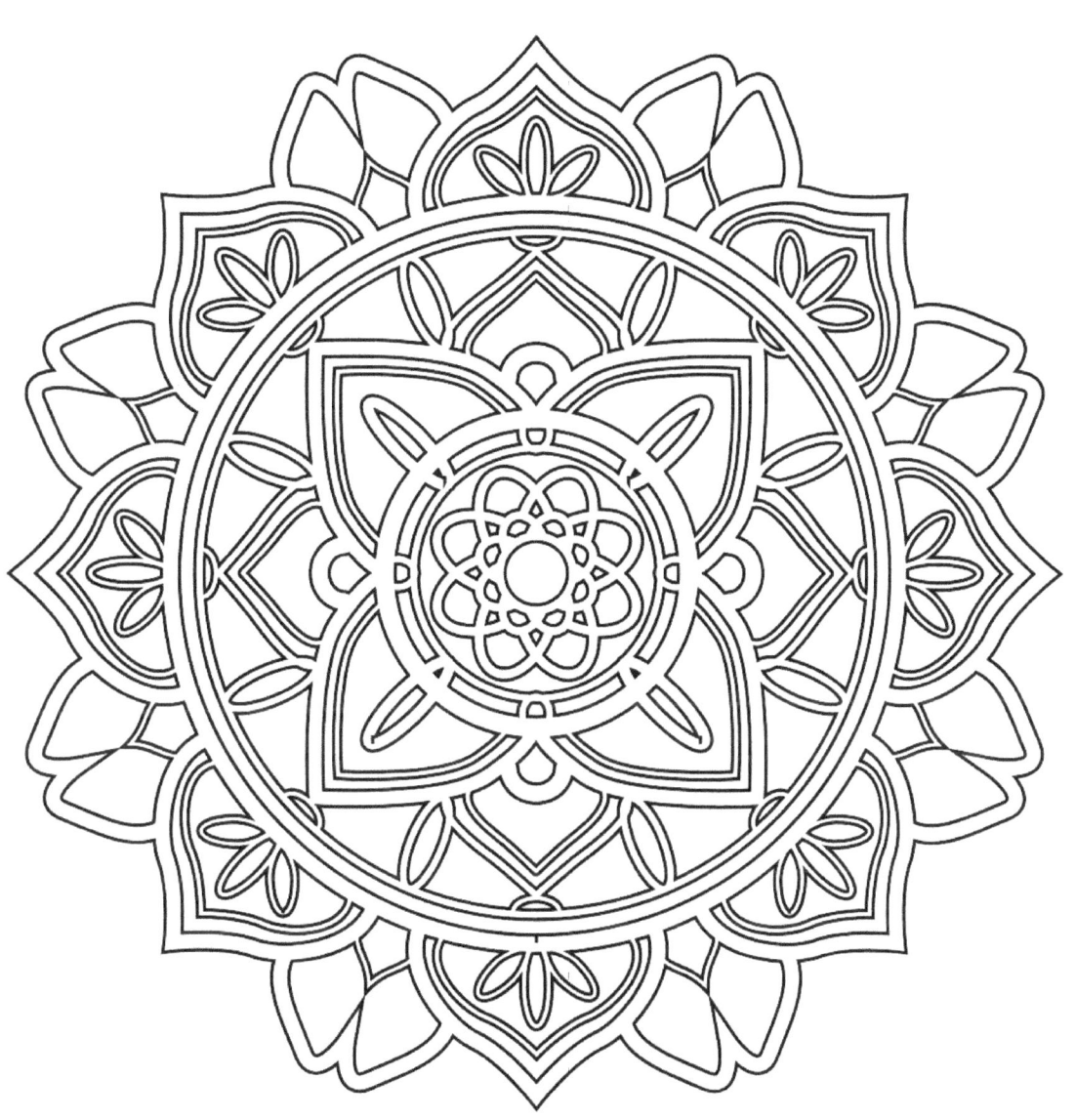